MW01106969

Sa

Florida Panther

By Steven Otfinoski

Contents

A Magnificent Animal 2

Behavior 4

Hunting for Food 5

The Panther's Past 6

Protecting the Panther at Last 9

Putting Collars on Panthers 11

Special Dangers to Panthers 16

More Recovery Efforts 19

Breeding with Texas Cougars 21

Hope for the Future 23

Glossary . . . . Inside Back Cover

Celebration Press
Pearson Learning Group

A Magnificent Animal

Some people call it a panther. Others call it a cougar, and still others say it's a mountain lion. No matter which name you choose, the Florida panther is a magnificent animal.

The Florida panther is a member of the cat family, *Felidae*, which also includes the cougar. The Florida panther is actually one of more than 20 types, or **subspecies**, of cougar. It is the only cougar known to live east of the Mississippi River.

The Florida panther is neither the largest nor the smallest of the cougars. A male panther grows to about 7 feet long from nose to tail tip and can weigh as much as 160 pounds. Females are somewhat smaller and weigh up to 100 pounds.

The panther's coat is usually reddish- or yellowish-brown or gray. Its chest, underbelly, and inner legs are lighter in color. This description would also fit the western cougar, but the panther has two other important features that help set it apart. It has a funny **cowlick** (a small bunch of hair that will not lie flat) in the middle of its back. It also has a kink at the end of its tail.

Close-up of the cowlick on a panther's back

Behavior

The Florida panther needs a great deal of land to roam in. Each male ranges over about 150 to 300 square miles. (An area of land 20 miles long by 15 miles wide is 300 square miles. That's equal to about one-quarter of the entire state of Rhode Island.)

To mark the border of its territory, the panther makes small piles of dirt and leaves called "**scrapes**." If another male should cross this border, the first panther will drive it away.

Panther making a scrape to mark its territory

Hunting for Food

When it comes to hunting, the Florida panther tends to rest by day and hunt its **prey** by night. It likes to eat white-tailed deer and wild hogs. It will also eat smaller animals such as raccoons and rabbits.

The panther can run up to 35 miles per hour for short distances. However, it prefers to surprise its prey rather than chase it for long distances. The panther draws close and then springs on the prey. It may kill the animal by biting the back of its neck, cutting the spinal cord. It may also bite its prey's throat, stopping its breath.

The Panther's Past

The Florida panther and other wild cats once roamed the southeastern United States. Native Americans respected the panther. Some tribes may have even worshiped it. This "panther man" statue was discovered in Florida in 1896. Scientists believe it is at least 500 years old.

However, Europeans who settled the eastern United States felt differently about the panther. They feared it would attack them and their farm animals, so they shot panthers on sight. In the 1800s the state of Florida paid people money for killing panthers. By 1897 the amount was five dollars for a panther scalp, which in those days was a lot of money.

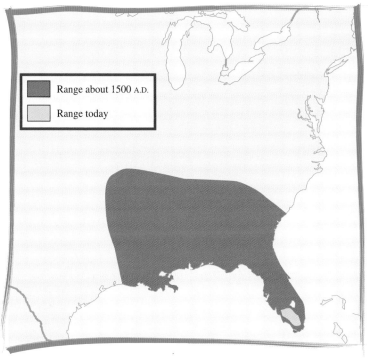

The **range** of the Florida panther has decreased greatly since the 1500s.

Gradually, people crowded the panther out of its habitat. Much of the open land on which the panther once roamed was turned into farmland. Citrus trees and vegetable crops, which made a lot of money for the landowners, were planted.

The panther was forced to retreat farther and farther south. Finally it found refuge in the remote swamps of the Florida Everglades.

In 1958 the state of Florida recognized that the panther was in danger and passed laws to protect it. Fifteen years later the panther was recognized as an **endangered species,** a type of animal or plant in danger of becoming extinct, or dying out.

But by this time, many felt it was too late. Few people had seen a panther in years. Were they all dead?

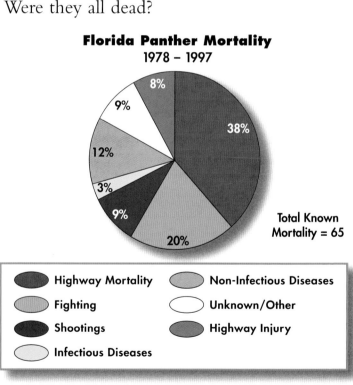

Florida Panther Mortality
1978 – 1997

38%

8%

9%

12%

3%

9%

20%

Total Known
Mortality = 65

Highway Mortality   Non-Infectious Diseases

Fighting   Unknown/Other

Shootings   Highway Injury

Infectious Diseases

Protecting the Panther at Last

To find the answer, the U.S. Fish and Wildlife Service formed a Panther Recovery Team. Its first job was to search for living panthers and learn all about them.

Why should people care about saving the Florida panther? For one thing the panther is a beautiful animal. It is one of the great cats of the world. To lose it would be a great loss. But there are more practical reasons for saving the panther.

The panther is a rare and beautiful animal.

This panther has captured a fawn.

The Florida panther is at the top of the food chain. It helps control the populations of deer, wild hogs, and raccoons. Without the panther these animal populations would multiply to enormous numbers and become a problem for humans.

Usually the panther kills only those animals that are sick or old. In this way it helps keep the population of its prey healthy. The panther also keeps deer on the run, which keeps the deer from overgrazing the land.

Putting Collars on Panthers

The Florida Panther Recovery Team looked for signs of the panther, especially in the Big Cypress and Everglades areas of southern Florida. They found paw prints, scrapes, and the remains of eaten animals.

After more searching the team found three separate groups of panthers. They counted between 30 and 50 adult panthers altogether. This small population made the Florida panther one of the most endangered animals in the world.

The recovery team needed more information about this shy animal in order to save it. To get information, they needed to capture each panther and examine it. Then they would put a collar on the panther and release it back into the wild.

Each collar had a radio built into it. The radio gave off signals that could be picked up by the recovery team.

So how do you get close enough to a wild panther to put a collar around its neck? It isn't easy!

The scientists enter a panther area, usually at sunrise. They bring along special equipment and hunting dogs. The dogs track down a panther, which tries to escape by climbing up a tree. Next the scientists put a large air-filled cushion under the tree. Then they hang a rope net in the tree above the cushion.

A veterinarian "shoots" the panther with a dart containing medicine. The medicine enters the animal's body and makes it fall asleep for a short while.

The radio collar on this young panther's neck will send out signals that tell its location.

This panther has landed safely in an air-filled cushion.

Then the panther either falls into the net or is lowered down from the tree with ropes. The scientists examine the panther for injuries and illnesses and treat it with medicine if necessary. They weigh it and give it shots to prevent rabies and other common diseases. Then they draw some of its blood for testing.

Before the panther awakens, the radio collar is put on its neck. Each radio collar has its own signal. Team members often go up in airplanes to pick up the animal's signal. They can track a panther's movement and tell its location. They can even tell when it meets another panther. A certain signal will tell them if the animal is dead. Then they try to recover the dead panther and study it to learn how and why it died.

A team of workers checks out a captured panther and places a radio collar around its neck.

Special Dangers to Panthers

Florida panthers die from many things. Some die from disease or illness. Some are killed in fights with other panthers. Between 1978 and 1994 many panthers were struck and killed by cars when crossing highways.

One of these highways cuts across the state. It is called Alligator Alley because it passes through the Everglades where there are many alligators.

When Alligator Alley became Interstate Highway 75 in the early 1990s, the state of Florida built **underpasses** designed to let panthers and other animals cross under the roadway safely. Tall fences on either side of the highway now guide the animals to the underpasses.

Interstate Highway 75, known as Alligator Alley, passes through panther territory.

A panther using an underpass
to cross under a highway

Special cameras were
set up to photograph
the underpasses to see if
they were working. The photos
showed that panthers, alligators, and bobcats
were all using them. Since the underpasses
have been built, no panthers have been killed
by cars or trucks.

More Recovery Efforts

In spite of many successes, still more efforts were needed to save the panther. In 1982 the state named the Florida panther its official animal. All residents could now take pride in this beautiful animal and help to save it.

But it will take more than highway underpasses and radio collars to save the Florida panther. The few panthers left have been so isolated that they have been "**inbreeding**" for years.

Inbreeding takes place when related panthers mate. As a result, their offspring are often born with severe problems. Because of inbreeding, many surviving panthers have poor health, such as holes in their hearts. Others cannot reproduce.

The U.S. Fish and Wildlife Service wanted to improve the panthers' health and increase their chances for survival, so it began a captive-breeding program in 1991.

Scientists captured ten panther kittens— five males and five females. The kittens were unrelated and were captured in a variety of places. They were very well cared for. Their keepers wanted the captured kittens to live as freely as they would in the wild, so they had only limited contact with humans.

The goal was to have a number of healthy panthers born to the captive panthers and to release the young panthers back into the wild. However, because of problems with breeding and some resistance to the plan, the program so far has not been successful.

Breeding with Texas Cougars

In the 1990s, scientists decided to try still another way to save the Florida panther. They had panthers mate with other subspecies of cougar to produce healthier young. Such inter-species breeding had taken place for centuries. But for many years the panthers have been isolated in southern Florida, which has prevented such breeding with close relatives.

An adult Texas cougar

Scientists decided to breed the Florida panther with the Texas cougar, a close relative. This cougar has survived well in its home state.

Recently a group of Texas cougars were brought to Florida and released into the wild. Some of the female cougars have mated with the male panthers and produced healthy offspring.

A Texas cougar being released into the Florida wilderness

Hope for the Future

Florida has been working hard to save its last great **predator**. But are these efforts enough?

If efforts are successful and the panther population continues to grow, the animals will need more land. Outside of the Everglades most of the forested land is gone. It has been developed for homes, farms, and shopping centers. Even within the Everglades, the Florida panther is losing needed roaming ground. Since 1948 many acres of this national park have been drained and developed.

There are many efforts now underway to save the panther. Florida has set up programs to buy public land. Private groups cooperate by buying land and giving it to the state. Having this new, protected land will help the panther to survive.

This panther kitten needs room to roam.

Late in 2000, President Clinton signed into law the Everglades Restoration Plan. It is a 30-year plan that will provide money to restore about 2 million acres and help protect the habitat of many endangered species, including the Florida panther and the West Indian manatee.

Only constant effort and new ideas and technology will help the Florida panther survive. It is up to all of us to help save this rare and beautiful animal. With hard work and luck, the panther may survive the 21st century and beyond.